T0147032

Titles by *L*

Forest Echoes

(Poems)

Nol Alembong

Langaa Research & Publishing CIG
Mankon, Bamenda

Publisher:
Langaa RPCIG
Langaa Research & Publishing Common Initiative
Group
P.O. Box 902 Mankon
Bamenda
North West Region
Cameroon
Langaagrp@gmail.com
www.langaa-rpcig.net

Distributed outside N. America by African Books
Collective
orders@africanbookscollective.com
www.africanbookscollective.com

Distributed in N. America by Michigan State
University Press
msupress@msu.edu
www.msupress.msu.edu

ISBN: 9956-616-36-2

© Nol Alembong 2010

DISCLAIMER

The names, characters, places and incidents in this book are either the product of the author's imagination or are used fictitiously. Accordingly, any resemblance to actual persons, living or dead, events, or locales is entirely one of incredible coincidence.

Contents

"One who enters the forest does not listen to the breaking of the twigs in the brush."

Bemba (Zambia) Proverb

Introduction

Poetry's fluid, if not elusive, nature when it comes to its definition, confirms that it has meant so many different things and served so many varied purposes to so many sundry peoples and generations alike in the course of history; the story is no different today. Mindful of this volume's wide-ranging themes and the different stylistic approaches Nol Alembong uses, his *Forest Echoes* is a literary quilt revealing a mature poet bestriding generations as he patches together a people's culture, their philosophy, history, along with their attendant woes into a subtle, sometimes disillusioning even, yet purposeful and poignant whole.

Nol Alembong is not afraid to be himself in this work: a scholar, teacher, parent, traditionalist and, above all, an Anglophone-Cameroonian. Whatever the case, these are magisterial and equally influential individual traits that have merged into a united whole in forging this poet's identity and concerns as evident from the thematic panorama of *Forest Echoes*. In "Forest Echoes", the title poem, for example, one encounters a poet who, though steeped in his people's struggles, has been able to stand back, watch and evaluate the effects of the interactions of time, events, and society. It is this ability of his, as an involved yet detached observer, along with the trend of events that have scarred his people's lives, which have yielded the powerful emotions that he has assembled in this thematically lush, historically nostalgic, and overwhelmingly evocative collection.

Thematically, Alembong explores, amongst others, his country's history before escaping into the sacred grove of culture to console and reassure himself about his identity and potentials. One of Alembong's primary concerns is the gruelling Anglophone predicament in today's Cameroon which has also been pivotal in numerous literary opuses coming out of Anglophone-Cameroon today, the genre notwithstanding. Consequently, Alembong sometimes emerges as an embittered poet trying to make sense of life, primarily as a Cameroonian, and then as an African. Accordingly, he begins by celebrating life and its complications in "Forest" which hinges on the philosophical implications of appearance and reality as things are not what they seem to be at a first glance and especially from afar. A closer encounter with events and scenarios reveal otherwise as one tends to see, hear, grasp, and in fact sense the truth which is different from what it had appeared to be from afar. To Alembong, in other words, his society is like a forest which, from afar, looks "dense", "green", like "a chorus", and "the home of plants", but a closer look reveals cracks, unsuspected rows, and a camouflaged discordance.

In lamenting the consequences of colonialism on Africa, the poet's agrarian image is effective as one can imagine colonialism as this huge and imposing tree which has left its roots deep down in the fertile substratum of Africa's cultural strata. The result is the poet's disillusionment with the reunification of Cameroon, by which colonialist-orchestrated exercise Southern Cameroons and La République du Cameroun merged to form one nation. It is this same disillusionment that caused the late vitriolic Anglophone-Cameroonian man of letters, Bate Besong, to christen the emerging Southern Cameroonian population "beasts of no nation". Alembong laments consequently in "Forest Echoes":

> We crossed the river with our heads high,
> As high as baobab leaves that tower the forest.
> We crossed to meet our brothers, so we thought,
> And there it dawned on us that a brother's punch
> Is harder to bear than that of a stranger.
> We crossed to meet our friends, so we thought,
> And there it dawned on us that no one
> Counts the teeth in the mouth of a friend's dog.

We crossed to form as great union, so we thought,
And there it dawned on us that a wise man does not
Measure his footprints with those of an elephant. (p.11)

Regret could hardly be presented in a more concrete form than indicated by these lines, yet this is the tone in all of this poem and more in the volume. After crossing and "Living East of the Mungo", to reunite with La République du Cameroun, it dawned on the poet, even as he is "Remembering February 11, 1961", the date of the plebiscite that led to the reunification, that Cameroon's journey from her days as a United Nations' protectorate to a republic today, amounts to some as an exercise in futility. Reunification only seemed to have served as a stage in what I had earlier described elsewhere as the "horizontal colonization" of Southern Cameroons by a French-backed majority. Alembong reiterates this by revealing the unpatriotic hypocrites our politicians have been in "The Democrat and his Fans" and "The Sin of Glory" for example. His disgust at these politicians and those around them is effectively captured in "The New Prophets". It is no wonder then, that "Sleep Walking" is reminiscent of the chaotic society depicted in Charles Dickens's *Bleak House*. It is thus a disenchanted and frustrated poet who thought his people crossed the Mungo to meet with "brothers".

However, from time to time, Alembong seizes the opportunity to re-energize himself and point out the way to a better tomorrow. He does this by celebrating Bamenda, for example, for always keeping in check the irresponsible excesses of bastardized regimes determined to transform the nation into a wasteland. That he may not choke on his own anger at the disheartening outcome of the reunification, the poet moves on to lighter concerns with far less traumatizing and importunate appeals, comparatively speaking, as encountered in "Saturday Nights off Campus" which echoes Emmanuel Fru Doh's "Life on Campus" and "Asumpta" which brings to mind Okot p'Bitek's "Song of Lawino". Beyond this, there is a lot more thematically, such as praise for the poet's homeland in "Lebialem" which has a line, "before you, naked we stand", echoing Christopher Okigbo in "Heavensgate". In the same blithe manner, the poet goes on to explore the effects of people's accents on speech in "Speaking". With such a broad spectrum of subjects explored, the poet's effort is thematically rich and equally as serious as it cries out for attention from his readers.

Alembong's technique, on the other hand, is cogent and superbly refreshing as all too often the traditionalist that he is comes to the fore. Typical of oral traditions, a poem like "Forest Echoes", which has a narrator and a chorus to answer back to the narrator's solo utterances, can be performed. At other moments, Alembong's use of proverbs to establish himself an authority over all that he is lamenting about, and the frequent employment of formulae, local diction, and the structure of oral narratives is a confirmation of the heavy influence of the oral tradition in his work. In "Asumpta" for example, the village wonders about this westernized girl:

How would she pick the jiggers in his father's feet?
How would she pick the lice in his mother's hair?
How would she mop his brother's floor?
How would she court his sister…? (p.35)

In the same vein, consider the messages being given a diseased person which also serve as prayers to the persona's ancestors in the dirge "Cycles":

Go in peace to the home of Mankem.
Tell Njingu we continue to look up to him.
Tell Lekeateh Ateng'a Lekang has swallowed itself.
Tell Tanjo'nji Aduiiha-nkeng had long developed legs.
Tell Asongtia our goats no longer produce triplets.

Ask Abouatmboh to send us more cows.
Join them in looking after us
Until the fire on our hilltops burns out (p.47)

This is typical of the oral traditions of Africa. Alembong, consequently, may be living in an hour tormented by a clash of cultures as a result of colonialism, neo-colonialism, and today's globalization, but he has refused to forget his roots. His poetry, accordingly, is heavily laced with his traditional worldview as encountered in "Song of Awambeh" and "Tekwombuo" even as he jostles, sparingly though, with alienating consequences of the colonial encounter which are exposed when he relapses into biblical and other western imagery, diction, and syntax. Consider "verily verily, in "The Democrat and His Fans", or "Camelot" in "Bridging the Atlantic". His heavy dependence on traditional oral techniques, like the use of proverbs, oral formulae, and specialized traditional enunciation gives more flavour to Alembong's poetry. This is in spite of the bitter truth about his people's predicament which ends up according the work a Cameroonian, and typically African essence. Alembong is, therefore, a skilled bard who, with confidence, leads his audience lyrically from the awkwardness of modern day socio-political treachery into the refreshing and trusting arms of tradition, the fertile native soil in which the acute beauty of this volume is rooted. Stylistically, *Forest Echoes* is a celebration of the poet's culture and his identity, his regrets and his hopes. Alembong basks in the beauty of his "native" language and worldview as he applies enlightening proverbs, like balm, to uplift and soothe his tortured environment.

In sum, Nol Alembong's work, remarkably, continues to grow in thematic complexity and stylistic beauty and sophistication as his effort in *Forest Echoes* displays an oeuvre which explores the painful and equally challenging double consciousness required and typical of an Anglophone-

Cameroonian in an effort to establish and maintain his or her identity and sanity in Cameroon today. Whether speaking softly or shouting as is typical of some of his poetic voices, the poems in this stunning volume urge one to look closely at one's world in a bid to improve upon the oppressed lot of so many unacknowledged victims. These, therefore, are poems that bear witness to a troubled poet as they chronicle him taking stock of his people's plight even as they, like Asumpta in "Asumpta", continue to drift away from their roots in pursuit of alien values that all too often conjure up disaster for remuneration. As a Cameroonian, Alembong is aware of the historical vicissitudes that rear bitterness, hatred, and violence in a people who ought to be one, had the tragedy titled "colonialism" not been plotted and acted out.

This volume confirms Alembong as a poet who is conscious of his surroundings; a poet whose tender patriotic feelings are blighted by historical strides that amount to his people's woes. It is the plight of his people that Alembong laments all too often even as he revamps his convictions about what ought to have been, and what has to be, through a rich style which pays tribute to his culture's noble values. Greatly troubled by man's deeds to man, Alembong can only find temporary solace in traditional wisdom as he counsels others while praying for better days in a manner redolent of the untroubled years of yore before Stanley met Mutesa.

Emmanuel Fru Doh
Minnesota, USA,
July, 13th, 2009

The Beginning

In the beginning was the forest,
The forest was with the earth,
The forest was the earth.

The forest was one.
It had one head.
It had one mouth.
It had one eye.
It had one ear.

But the fire came,
The fire came…

Forest

A forest is dense
To those who see it from without;
When in, we see
The position of each tree.

A forest is green
To those who see it from without;
When in, we see
The colour of each tree.

A forest is a chorus
To those who listen from without;
When in, we hear
Each tree singing its own song.

A forest is the home of plants
To those who see it from without;
When in, we find
Nests and the trails of beasts.

A forest is a jungle
To those who see it from without;
When in, we learn that
The bamboo that tries to rub shoulders with the mahogany
Will find it brought down by the wind.

A forest is a jungle
To those who see it from without;
When in, we learn that
The parrot will lose its eyes to the night
Should it try to mimic the owl.

A forest is a jungle
To those who see it from without;
When in, we learn that
Bugs suck to live, not to kill,
As bees sting to give, not to take.

Forest Echoes

POET:
Wife's food still a-cooking
Son and daughter at arm's length –
Nailed to their bamboo stools,
Scourged by fetters of smoke
And the thirst for lore –
He chose to pass the time
In song and story:
The tale of old and new.

CHORUS:
When will our streams flow to their cradle
And leave the Seine to its stony ways?
When will our fishes gather in the great pond
And leave preying hawks to feast on fires?

POET:
Voice cleared –
The way our birds clear their throats
To sing the song of dawn, to make
Sleep leave our heads –
The tale hung on his lips, ripe for harvest
Like pointed breasts for sucking.

CHORUS:
When will our streams flow to their cradle
And leave the Seine to its stony ways?
When will our fishes gather in the great pond
And leave preying hawks to feast on fires?

POET:
Outside,
The sky tore its garment open
And unleashed a dark fog over the land.
Outside,
Haunting phrases of wailing owls
Rescued the land to misery.
Outside,
The hen and the partridge passed for one another,
As the pig and the boar the same.
Outside,
Unshod feet smashed their homeward ways,
Embracing the fog like the hen her chicks.
Outside,
The land was enveloped like walnuts in their shells
And birds slept with their eyes open.

CHORUS:
When will our streams flow to their cradle
And leave the Seine to its stony ways?
When will our fishes gather in the great pond
And leave preying hawks to feast on fires?

POET:
Inside,
Heads were being cleared for the tale
The way our mothers prepare farm plots
For the harvest sun.
Inside,
A hen went to the stream alone
But returned with many chicks:
They said it was a sown groundnut seed
That germinated to produce many more.
Inside,
A leaf dropped into a pool

And became a tadpole:
They said it was blood
That became a child in a woman.
Inside,
A man looked like a small house,
A small house with a big roof:
They said he was a palm tree,
A palm tree left unpruned.

CHORUS:
When will our streams flow to their cradle
And leave the Seine to its stony ways?
When will our fishes gather in the great pond
And leave preying hawks to feast on fires?

NARRATOR:
A river it was that lay between us —
The placing the Creator's, as though an injunction…
As though an injunction against trespass.
And the hurricane came, and the river became mire.
So we lived as though one, with a cyclone round us.
We lived and worked for these stranger-masters:
We built houses for their sun-baked bodies
We built shrines for their unknown ancestors
We built roads for their moving houses.
Then a war broke out in their countries
And it reached us like a tornado our cornfields.
A dog that does not know its master
Must not be used for hunting.
They thought we knew them, and so they used us.

CHORUS:
When will our streams flow to their cradle
And leave the Seine to its stony ways?
When will our fishes gather in the great pond
And leave preying hawks to feast on fires?

NARRATOR:
At last they fell, like baobab chopped by fire.
Ah! To cut a tree may not be the end of the tree,
For its roots still breathe in the soil
And can send forth shoots to take its place.
And as a dog always returns to its vomit
So did other sun-baked skins emerge
To take the place of our stranger-masters
But they spoke in two tongues, these new comers,
And so thought our sky was spacious enough
For one bird not to disturb the other.
That's why the mire went and the river returned.
That's why the two sides of the river each had a tongue.
That's why the one went to the Seine for water
And the other, for true, to the Thames.

CHORUS:
When will our streams flow to their cradle
And leave the Seine to its stony ways?
When will our fishes gather in the great pond
And leave preying hawks to feast on fires?

NARRATOR:
That's why they cannot eat their ears in conversation
With one another – they must use the drum.
That's why each side fought its strangers for survival,
Forgetting the lore of the land, forgetting that
A masquerade that wanders alone
Will have his face exposed.
They fought separately and won each its fight.
And their skies were freed from the haunting presence
Of the Tricolour and the Union Jack.
The termite is wise; it uses its head to build.
The cobra is wise; it uses its head to kill.
So it was when our land became ours again
So it was when our sons replaced the strangers

Who had cut through us as goats in an abattoir.
And so we had rams fastened to stakes,
We had fowls slaughtered at cross-roads,
We had ground melon seeds sprinkled along footpaths,
We had oil and salt on the lips of all in the land
And we all raised our voices to our gods
That this may pass as dreams through the head –
For does morning not show what evening will be?
But as a bird of prey is not known for dying young
So did cobras live to slacken the people's muscles
While termites were eager to leave anthills behind.
A river it was that divided the land,
And both sides with each a tongue.
But as the thumb must join the fingers
In the courtyard for fear of death
So was the West made to stick to the East bank
And our bushes eaten up by fire,
And our streams forced to change their course.

CHORUS:
When will our streams flow to their cradle
And leave the Seine to its stony ways?
When will our fishes gather in the great pond
And leave preying hawks to feast on fires?

NARRATOR:
Fire cannot cross a river without broken reeds.
Streams don't go off course without having been
rechannelled.
And so two chiefdoms were fused into a gauge
The way a mole's hole is stuffed with dried reeds
In preparation for a mole hunt.
And so two hills were lost to the fog
And in their place stood a peak of fog.
The bee is a friend, its honey is sweet.
The viper is a foe, its venom is bitter.

CHORUS:
When will our streams flow to their cradle
And leave the Seine to its stony ways?
When will our fishes gather in the great pond
And leave preying hawks to feast on fires?

NARRATOR:
One should not hate the head to the extent
Of putting the cap on the buttocks.
The cap is to the head what
The Opposition is to the Government.
This version of truth was betrayed, and
Sacrificed by Her Majesty's Government
Unknown to Her Majesty's Opposition itself.
They had our votes, but betrayed our blood.
If one is made the chief of hawks
He should be able to catch chickens
Even if he will need the help of his opponents –
For a bird cannot fly with one arm.

CHORUS:
When will our streams flow to their cradle
And leave the Seine to its stony ways?
When will our fishes gather in the great pond
And leave preying hawks to feast on fires?

NARRATOR:
When a child defecates in the house at night
He thinks the day will not break.
Our flag bearers left filth
In the conference room
For they thought a roof was over their heads.
Ours was the land, ours the future
But both were offered in return for
Daughters for children.

And when the sun shone over our heads
It dawned on us that the frog
Does not have as much knowledge
Of the river as the fish.
But who were we to say so?
If the fox has a boil in the mouth
It is not the fowl to point it out.

CHORUS:
When will our streams flow to their cradle
And leave the Seine to its stony ways?
When will our fishes gather in the great pond
And leave preying hawks to feast on fires?

NARRATOR:
Get a wife in haste so that you may have no wife.
So did it happen to some who bore our banners.
They crossed the river and what we stood for
Crossed their heads.
Little did they know that the river
That forgets its source will dry up.
No sooner did they settle on their new jobs
Than their masters began to use partridges
For sacrifice in the place of hens.

CHORUS:
When will our streams flow to their cradle
And leave the Seine to its stony ways?
When will our fishes gather in the great pond
And leave preying hawks to feast on fires?

NARRATOR:
The termite is wise; it uses its head to build.
The cobra is wise; it uses its head to kill.

CHORUS:
When will our streams flow to their cradle
And leave the Seine to its stony ways?
When will our fishes gather in the great pond
And leave preying hawks to feast on fires?

NARRATOR:
The bee is a friend, its honey is sweet.
The viper is a foe, its venom is bitter.

CHORUS:
When will our streams flow to their cradle
And leave the Seine to its stony ways?
When will our fishes gather in the great pond
And leave preying hawks to feast on fires?

NARRATOR:
We crossed the river with our heads high,
As high as baobab leaves that tower the forest.
We crossed to meet our brothers, so we thought,
And there it dawned on us that a brother's punch
Is harder to bear than that of a stranger.
We crossed to meet our friends, so we thought,
And there it dawned on us that no one
Counts the teeth in the mouth of a friend's dog.
We crossed to form a great union, so we thought,
And there it dawned on us that a wise man does not
Measure his footprints with those of an elephant.

CHORUS:
When will our streams flow to their cradle
And leave the Seine to its stony ways?
When will our fishes gather in the great pond
And leave preying hawks to feast on fires?

NARRATOR:
We crossed because of the urge to retrace our roots
Oblivious of the fact that it is on its old trail
That an animal meets its death.
For since we crossed
Our sun's face has turned grey.
Since we crossed
Our moon no longer appears at night.
Since we crossed
Our sky has worn a black veil.
Since we crossed
 Our birds no longer sing in different ways.
Since we crossed
Our seedlings have never seen the harvest sun.
Since we crossed
Our roads have become the ant's trail.
Since we crossed
Our farms have been seized by locusts.

CHORUS:
When will our streams flow to their cradle
And leave the Seine to its stony ways?
When will our fishes gather in the great pond
And leave preying hawks to feast on fires?

NARRATOR:
The bee is a friend, its honey is sweet.
The viper is a foe, its venom is bitter.

CHORUS:
When will our streams flow to their cradle
And leave the Seine to its stony ways?
When will our fishes gather in the great pond
And leave preying hawks to feast on fires?

POET:
No one can stop termites from leaving the earth.
The road to harvest mushroom is never too long for one.
It is a fool who thinks he can kill a snake with a broom
stick.

CHORUS:
When will our streams flow to their cradle
And leave the Seine to its stony ways?
When will our fishes gather in the great pond
And leave preying hawks to feast on fires?

The Crossing

Glow-wormed skies
Sank on the threshold
Of pebbled shores;
Green hope raced
Out of the sheath
Of silver memories;
Then…

Then the waves came,
Tossed the travellers
On the lance bridge,
Made them chickens
Out of doors at roost time
Or streamline mimosa
In shunning fits.

Near the other side…
Water and bridge were caught
In a frantic love dance;
Grey seasons hung stiff,
Nose-length away,
And: a waterfall silence –
Tongue of a statue!

Then
Neon threads lit the horizon
With serpentine agitation
Showing the gateway to
One of Africa's Frog Republics.

And
A dog-nose coldness
Seized the newcomers' ribs
At the thought of giving up oysters
For a meal of toads.

Living East of the Mungo

I rose with the cock's crow
As with sunlight crops grow
And saw the path that I must
Take to get out of the dust.

But the dust swallowed me up
As palm-wine overflows a cup
For the path was of naked earth
This to the woe of our commonwealth

And when I trod this common path
And emerged from my dusty bath
Then did I know that loving tonic
That taught me never again to panic.

Remembering February 11, 1961

End:
>Follow me across the western line
>And yonder find the majestic Niger –
>The Lethe to our imbroglio,
>And yonder find the high-rise –
>The lift to the equinox;
>And yonder find oil shores –
>The spark plugs for our bleak lives.

Fon:
>It's a foolish man who measures
>His footprints with those of the elephant.
>From across the Mungo's eastern bank
>The rising sun shall for ever fuel our lives,
>Pollen shall bud our evergreen fields,
>Eels shall throng our streams,
>And fraternal love shall cap our gains.

Voice (ex machina)
>The West stands in wait, the East too,
>Of a lamb for the shrine
>Be not the Blue Nile that sacrifices
>Its multiple gains to mother Nile.
>Go not with the common run,
>Go alone and leave a trail,
>Go alone and leave a trail.

The Democrat and His Fans

Like spirit-maidens
he danced at noon,
on the threshold of pain.

Caught in mid-throb limping,
unable to get the rhythm right,
he settled on his own urine.

The music became hemlock
to the best of fans, and daily
he lost his feathers to the chill.

With warm clothing from across the seas
and paid gun-men at vantage points
came the time for harvest reports:

Abattoirs have sunk into the earth,
other dance groups have sprung up in the land,
and birds now sing true to their types.

And licences came from across the seas
to enable the mole deepen our debt-wells
and stamp more wrinkles on our faces.

And more tentacles came from across the seas
to enable the octopus pluck us from up-stream dwellings
and add more skulls to the home of death.

And some strychnine came from across the seas
to enable the kingfisher have an easy catch
for fear of eating crabs when fishes rush into crannies.

17

And more fibre came from across the seas
to enable the hawk catch more chicks
and maim cocks from crowing in eggs.

But why keep the hawk and reject the dove
when one day of rain is better than
one thousand days of drought?

Verily, verily,
one day of rain is better than
one thousand days of drought.

The Sin to Glory

He mounted the rostrum,
Fist clenched, and the punched air
Received his loud promises.

Their paths to bliss would see
A metal tar on every inch
If he were spun into
The hole of the roulette.

With conquered votes in hand
His stomach began to fall over his belt
While their hearts were being sucked dry
Of the last drop of hope.

Who said one mounts a horse
To spur it to his own doom?
'Tis for game a vulture perches.

The New Prophets

Clear like crystals
from a baptismal anvil,
fire bronzed riddles
in cave darkness,
the new prophets –
the generation's anodyne
(the people were told) –
took their turn – parading.

Quetzal beauties
on a podium of dew
with quizzical smiles
read the letters of their drug
in a bravura performance.

A rhetoric of whispering wind
in cornfields – soothing destitution.

Hooting owls at noon
capped the world with rusty moons
and the beaming moon
x-rayed the spotty prophets:
deodorizing furnaces
with promises of the moon;
golden quills above a harlot's forehead.

And the sputum from the podium
showed how healthy the nation was;
megalomaniac pomposity
showed how sane the people were.

The hooting over
and the fresh morning air
seized by the cock's cries
the promise of dawn
was on everyone's mind.

The Plague

It came
Like a millipede from a millpond,
Crawled on our sunbeams,
Crawled,
Crawled.

Snail-like
It felt its way
Into the womb of Mother Earth,
Nourishing her body
With slimy fluids.

O, how well the flowers blossomed
In the anthills of the savannah!
How stout mistletoe stood
On the irokos of the woodland!

Today,
Today,
Taproot chambers are filled with smut
And nascent roots nipped in fallopian tracks.

Tears

Tears
>   For the dove
>   Whose nestlings always disappear
>   After the viper's attack.

Tears
>   For the rodent
>   Whose underground world
>   Is often sacked by ferrets.

Tears
>   For the ewe
>   Whose lambs become the lion's faeces
>   After each invasion.

Tears
>   For the ploughman
>   Whose harvest often lies in waste
>   When the tempest is over.

Tears
>   For the scribe
>   Whose fecund pen
>   Is broken by neurotics.

Tears
>   For vampires and vandals
>   For little do they know
>   That flies side with ulcerous persons.

Sleepwalking

Silent
> As a vase
> Vomiting multiple
> Colours of the rainbow
> To enliven the bleak house:
> The post-Foumban Golgotha.

Silent
> As a photograph
> Laughing from grey walls
> At our cares in Hades;
> As a richly robed man in a picture
> Laughing at his ragamuffins.

Silent
> As a calendar
> Naming each passing day
> And calling us to the day's cares
> Else our sun sleeps at noon.

Silent
> As shelved books
> Shouting out our Foumban riddle –
> A riddle of caves and palaces –
> Mourning over our orphanhood
> Weeping for our neglected prawn land
> And for souls torn by broken promises.

Silent
> As fathomless sleep
> Rumbling in the depth of night
> The musings of the soul at morn
> And the body's cares at noon.

The Aerial Tour

The
air was seized
by wanton wasps,
like invading locusts
the angels of loss
filled the air.

And
the sacred horn released
the palm-wine of request
and the guardians of the land
urged to swallow the darkness
poured under our lamp-posts.

Then
the *Kuh-ngang* lords
with rituals staffs and statues
left the sacred grove
for the aerial tour –
For a cat and mouse game.

Now
we, handmaids of the grove,
await the promise of dawn,
the day of the dance, when
our sky will be cleared of miasma,
our farms of weeds,
our wombs of fibrosis,
and our lives hung once more
on steady sun beams.

Bamenda

Bamenda,
a land of smoking hills
where cattle for ever twine
in graceful meanderings.

Bamenda,
a land of smoking chimneys
lording stern looking roofs
in rustic elegance.

Bamenda,
heterodox people to some,
scathing tongues to others,
but Bamenda is Bamenda.

Bamenda,
the fetter for preying hawks
the trap for sly vampires
the insecticide for bedbugs.

Ah Bamenda!
«enfant terrible»!
the nation quakes when you hiss
and when you breathe it is at ease.

Bamenda,
our Athens,
our Marketplace,
our Sun!

Harvest Reports

Once more
Hailstones are singing the Eagle's songs
On the sleeping roofs in the woods...

This Lion is the cliff
That tumbles down sure waters.

This Lion is the scar
That wounds a girl's pride.

This Lion is the cataract
That deprives the woods of sunlight.

This Lion is the smoke
That cannot cook a pot.

This Lion is the weevil
That eats up beans in barns.

This Lion is the hawk
That makes mother hens run crooked.

This Lion is the viper
That swallows its own eggs.

This Lion is the locust
That stops crops from seeing the harvest sun.

This Lion is the singing bird
That cannot make a nest.

This Lion is the ant-lion
That builds on shifting sand.

And once more
The land is being rescued
From the jaws of lethargy.

And with insomniac grace
The dozy land catches
An eulogy in mid-throb…

The Eagle is the eye
That should not be blamed for seeing.

The Eagle is the mouth
That denounces rocks that
Make river currents fiercer…

With a harvest-call on their lips
The *Uhuru* cantors rinse the sleep
Out of the dark, silent woods.

Tug-of-war

Government:
    You are a plague of rats
    That ruins the nation the way
    Rats sack a barn of grain.
    Your 'ghost towns' crusade has
    Made the nation a colony of rats
    In church ceilings.
    Heed the call of Zacchaeus:
    Pay your taxes, so we may stay in business.

People:
    You are the crocodile
    That swallows its own eggs.
    The honey bee is wise:
    It sucks nectar but
    Leaves back pollen on the flower.
    Our wages run for months unpaid
    Because you're the crocodile, not the bee.
    Pay us, so we may pay our taxes.

Harvest Thanksgiving

Like a flood
the first verse
inundated our beings
in innuendo elegance:

There goes the bar and the Church
There goes spicy meat and His Body
There goes lager and His Blood
Isn't it said that He is the way
That leads to the Promised Land?

The second
hit the heavens
and echoed in the
womb of the earth:

Fear not an empty pocket
Fear not a home of lack
Fear not the future of the kids
Isn't it written in the Holy Book
That out of a rock Moses got water?

The indoor ritual over
stalls greeted the masses
with nimbus alertness
while the grandstand
warmly embraced the VIPs.

Surrounding green hills,
with perching houses of
the holy ones, looked on
in dumb-show…

Up went the bluff
of a pregnant man –
the chief tax collector
of the town – and
the applause of the VIPs –
his fart had become fine perfume:
he had pledged a month's pay.

Low went the weeping
and gnashing of teeth
of a skinny peasant
and the sighs of his brethren,
and the moan of his infants –
his sun had set at noon:
he had emptied his barn before the rains.

Back home
the harvest moon
beamed on the votaries
with green vengeance
and with dewy sparks.

Of Good and Bad Dogs

Kurd is a good dog
It stays hungry all day
Yet, with an empty tummy,
It gets hold of all thieves.

Bard is a bad dog
It eats its fill everyday
Still, with a full tummy,
It lets go all the thieves.

Saturday Nights off Campus

Dresses:
plumage of kingfishers
beaming in the tropical sun

Hair:
serpentine coils
like waves on the heads
of spirit maidens

Faces:
smeared with rainbow,
masking human grace
off celestial gardens

Mouths:
red plums sticking out
of ashen jaws
like bleeding haemorrhoids

And…
loud perfumes
to announce the spree.

Caves
open their tiny doors
to the galaxy of night birds,
single or accompanied,
they drift to the underworld
like cockroaches fleeing from light.

And there…
the bees go for the nectar
with slug felicity
and the daisies dim away
like a crimson sky at dusk.

Asumpta

She learnt how to cook books
Six harvests following her birth;
Since then she has been cooking books
For twenty more corn harvests.

The village wondered who she was,
This one whose room is full of books,
This one whose mother's barn is her bane,
This one of whom it is said

She learnt how to cook books
Six harvests following her birth;
Since then she has been cooking books
For twenty more corn harvests.

Who will marry her, people wondered,
This one who can't till for corn,
This one who can't pick out corn from cone,
This one of whom it is said

She learnt how to cook books
Six harvests following her birth;
Since then she has been cooking books
For twenty more corn harvests.

Her hair stood like the feathers of a mad hen,
Her face and neck baking in heavy powder,
Her outfit designed to define her body's contours,
This one of who it is said

She learnt how to cook books
Six harvests following her birth;
Since then she has been cooking books
For twenty more corn harvests.

The parrot thinks it can mimic,
The peacock believes it is bright,
The owl thinks it knows the night,
But Asumpta beats them all, for

She learnt how to cook books
Six harvests following her birth;
Since then she has been cooking books
For twenty more corn harvests.

Since the home of death does not lack skulls,
Neither is a dead goat too heavy for a thief to carry,
A lad got her in a haste, this who fell into her nest,
Got her in a haste so he may have no wife, for

She learnt how to cook books
Six harvests following her birth;
Since then she has been cooking books
For twenty more corn harvests.

The pair was the talk of the village,
This goose and his guinea fowl,
How would she cook for him?
How would she wash his clothes, since

She learnt how to cook books
Six harvests following her birth;
Since then she has been cooking books
For twenty more corn harvests.

How would she pick the jiggers in his father's feet?
How would she pick the lice in his mother's hair?
How would she mop his brother's floor?
How would she court his sister, since

She learnt how to cook books
Six harvests following her birth?
Since then she has been cooking books
For twenty more corn harvests.

Who said she was his father's wife?
Who said she was his mother's wife?
Who said she was whoever's wife?
Were questions on her bleeding lips, this one who

Learnt how to cook books
Six harvests following her birth; and
Since then she has been cooking books
For twenty more corn harvests.

Boy, hull the corn and pick the vegetables
While I get the rest ready
We have corn *fufu* for lunch today
Was her won't to say, this one who

Learnt how to cook books
Six harvests following her birth; and
Since then she has been cooking books
For twenty-five more corn harvests.

The cockerel danced and danced around the hen
Hopping on the right leg, then on the left one,
Knowing that today's seedlings are tomorrow's trees,
But no egg ever greeted his frantic effort, for

She learnt how to cook books
Six harvests following her birth;
Since then she has been cooking books
For thirty more corn harvests.

What are you doing with your mother?
What do you want from dried-up loins?
Can you find water in a rock?
Were songs about this one in the snare of one who

Learnt how to cook books
Six harvests following her birth; and
Since then she has been cooking books
For thirty-five more corn harvests.

It's not for offspring
That goats and sheep share a yard
Or horses and cows a field,
Was her won't to say, this one who

Learnt how to cook books
Six harvests following her birth; and
Since then she has been cooking books
For forty more corn harvests.

Lebialem

Lebialem sanctuary,
cave of caves,
a watery furnace,
quaffing for ever
the releases of sleeping hills.

From upland,
sleeping hills empty their bowels therein,
some with ease, some with speed,
with vaginal denial.

From upland,
peaks add their foggy crowns
to that of Lebialem
with reverential denial.

Lebialem!
like the Serpent god
you hiss by the hour
and trees from lowland and upland,
bow to let your breath pass.

Lebialem!
like the rain god
you shower surrounding countries with nectar,
and their wombs open to let it in
for the good of men, animals and plants.

Lebialem!
like a full bladder its content
you ejected the Betenten
and asked it to spread germ on its path
as it crawled to meet the Manyu, and both the sea.

Lebialem!
Spider!
see so that we may see.
before you, naked we stand,
arms stretched, hands open,
waiting for the dog's message
or that of the chameleon.

Bangwa Tiger (For E.A. Aka)

I

A colossal rippling
in deep, silent woods
caught sleeping embers
on the edge of a blade:
and there was silence.

Green hope rose to meet
raw sienna with catlike sprints
and spry pebbles spun to
empyreal heights:
and there were fireworks.

Spiral sparks
thawed the ashen night
and the face of the earth
unveiled with occult hands:
and there was dawn.

II

Dawn,
ruptures of rose buds
in celestial roof gardens.

Dawn,
scissures in sachets of beams
in the zodiac wheel.

Dawn,
a lullaby
for grey seasons.

III

And
Aurora's keen beams
clawed the spotless cub
with flaming smartness.

And
the towering woods
stood in girthful awe
of steaming reverence.

And
the rolling hills
greeted the stellar son
in graceful poise.

IV

The tiger
without a gong
pulled the woods to the marketplace.

The tiger
without a drum
sent the woods matching on.

The tiger
from low fields
traced the trail to the mountain top.

V

Today…

The sun
from yonder clouds
ripens ready grains
and prepares them
for the moist soil.

The moisture
from beneath the clay
buds the stalks
and prepares them
for the harvest sun.

To an Ambazonian Warrior

For you,
offspring of the elephant,
the slow-feet masquerades
ring the festival ground
in dumb-show…

Broad-leaved walking sticks
bridging ether and earth;

rattling feet
echoing the musings of the silent world…

For you,
baobab of the homestead,
the day has been put aside –
for ritual must raze to dust
our mountains of misty sighs.

Only three decades ago
lions went berserk
when a gun spoke in your hands.

Only three decades ago
palms bowed in ungirthly elegance
when drums screeched in your hands.

Only three decades ago
the land quirked
when you spoke in the marketplace.

Since you left,
rhinoceros of the highlands,
the fence trees have been eaten
by invading termites.

Since you left,
cat of the homestead,
mice have made our compounds
their play grounds.

Since you left,
fountainhead of the land,
streams have dried up
in the womb of Ambazonia.

For you
drum-beats weave the air
so that on the spider's thread
you can reach the ozone realm.

For you
the choirs cheer the silent ones
so that the hen should not pass
for the partridge.

For you
bare feet beat the festival ground
so that the meercat can give you
the leopard's skin.

To You, Florence

To you, Florence,
The gate is open wide,
Its path adorned with pearls,
Leading to poetry's cosy garden.

Therein, Florence,
Petals point to bright horizons,
Nectar, the freshness of your mind,
Stalks, the stoutness of your harvest.

With that, Florence
Light a candle in many a heart,
Brighten the horizon of many a soul,
Sweeten the lives of many a man.

And so, Florence,
Because of your poetry,
Green will ripen to orange,
And men will have a sweeter suck.

Cycles

Fonji-nya,
You are back to the earth,
The earth in whose hearth
Deep down the womb of our hills
Your human parts took form.

Today you have become earth.
Your flesh and the soil of your birth,
The soil that received your umbilical cord,
Are now one, like the wood and the statue,
Like the ant's spittle and the mud of the anthill,
In order that the fortress of our hope
May rise to touch the sky.

Well,
You are back to the earth
But the Fonship of Attah
Continues for ever, for ever,
For a forest never loses its lions.

It is strange, quite strange,
That the steam in the leopard
Has run out too soon;
That the fur on the tiger
Can no longer stand on end;
That the roar of the lion
Can no longer be heard on hill tops.

These are the wonders of the earth!
These are the things that prevent dogs,
Even the hunting dogs of chief hunters,
From smelling an animal's trail!
These are the things that turn the heads
Of the nine pillars of Attah!

Were it left to us,
Ten strong men,
Yes, men with the rhino's spine,
Would have been given in your place,
So that the leopard can continue to prowl the forest,
So that the hyena can continue to pile its spoils,
So that the lion can continue to chase foxes.

However,
As meat with fur cannot escape the fire's wrath,
So too life's steam can hardly avoid
The dog-nose coldness of the night.

Therefore,
Chart your way with the snail's feelers.
Leave behind as you glide
N*duat* in every home,
Dung on every farm plot,
Steam in the loins of every man,
Cold water in the womb of every woman.

Go in peace to the home of Mankem.
Tell Njingu we continue to look up to him.
Tell Lekeateh Ateng'a Lekang has swallowed itself.
Tell Tanjo'nji Aduiiha-nkeng had long developed legs.
Tell Asongtia our goats no longer produce triplets.
Ask Abouatmboh to send us more cows.
Join them in looking after us
Until the fire on our hilltops burns out.

Can the sun, dying of thirst,
Empty the water in the bowels of the rain?
Can thunder roar its approval of the moon
Sucking dry the wetness of the night?

The sun may set, but never does it sleep in Attah.
For Ntsie-che, the stream that burrows her womb,
Can dislodge her eels but not the eggs.
Ndem-mbo', the moulder of individual spirits,
Does not observe *Alung*, the day the lost ones are fed.
That is why the womb of *Mmah* Attah
Is always filled with cubs, cubs for the royal chair,
Hence the Fonship of Attah
Continues for ever, for ever,
Since a forest never loses its lions.

And so, from *Ndem-mbo*'s divine hands,
From his hearth in the womb of the earth,
From his pottery workshop, like *Bemuiteh* masquerades
Emerging from their mysterious palm-frond temples,
Came gliding, like the mighty one of the scrub land,
A cub for the stool, greeted by watery ululations.

And
The trumpeting of elephants,
The yapping of hyenas,
The howling of wolves,
Sent stones rolling uphill.

Could one have searched the mind for the riddle's answer?
It would have been like seeking to know
Why the fowl and not the partridge
Is used for sacrifice.
Or why the *suesue'a* plant and not *anzieh-mven*
Is used to bless newly married couples.

For,
Who knows the Great One who spits out Geleur,
The stream that joins Becheur at Abebue?
Who has ever seen the serpent that puffs out the fog

That keeps locusts at bay in Quibeku?
Who knows how Chichaba hill got its limestone?
Or how the Ngieh-Ngim range rose to lord it over Pia?
Who has ever seen the nipples below the Metet range
That produce the streams that irrigate Nzanchen?
How comes Kidsue cliff has deprived Ndung Essoh of fish?
Who has ever given meaning to Nwoh-Aleh's riddle?

A new day has dawned in Attah, dawned,
Without the sun having gone to sleep.
And now, drum beats echo in every heart,
Drum beats calling on Attah to go mushrooming in the
woods
Like pestle sounds do summon our appetite.

Ah!
In the village square
Alung-achaba masquerades
Dance on cobwebs
Like cats in a sprint show.

From a hill in watch
Amiliteh warriors file in,
Like ants dissecting a path,
Saluting the air with smoking guns.

Emerging from their *ndep*
Alung-ndeng'a dancers
Spin on bamboo tips
Like feathers being tossed on wind beams.

See how *nkeng* plants dance
On the tombs of the Ancients of Attah!
Hear how *Lefem* groves echo
The throb of sleeping tombs!

Ah!
Vapours now rise from Becheur falls
And eat up grey seasons on the Ngieh-Ngim range.
Nto'o from the horns of *begang-afu*
Now opens the eyes of sleeping masks.
Bang-mpfen on the floors of *begang-ngah*
Can now open the mouths of spiders.
Grains of light from *Belem* Attah
Now brighten the new dawn.

Dawn!
We wake to sleep again
And rise again to another dawn,
Like the bat that wakes with the moon
And sleeps so deep with the sun.

Bridging the Atlantic

Nimbus…
and the eagle
trod on Neptunian beams
to unveil the Camelot
in columbine lands.

Behind…
the greys and greens
hustle for the sun
while the bats and the owls
long for moonless nights.

Space…
effervescent embryonic spectacles,
floating realms of illusions,
bubbles of infantile creations
enveloping clay!

Welcome…
welcome, eagle,
welcome to New Farmland,
where falling acorns bud the oak
while stars fall on.

Speaking

When
some people speak through the nose
mud-guarding the dentist's gold teeth,
coating speech with sinusal mucus,
phlegming words at their roots,
and miming end tags

while
others speak through the mouth,
offering chisel-like teeth for scrutiny,
hail-stoning consonants on roof tops,
pecking words at their shoots,
and clattering end tags

do the receivers,
glued to their ears
for lack of a binding wire,
put them on the same wavelength?

Favourite Name

What is your favourite name?
The voice –
chill,
cream coated,
harp crescendo –
inquired.

Labyrinth.

I mean er…
What would you like to be called?

Faustian civility.

My name is Eteundem Aminkeng.
The other voice –
cocky,
palm-oil coated,
drum beat –
roared.

Labyrinth.

You get that?
I mean er…er…you understand?

A mosquito around the ear.

Lost.
Christian, nnou?

No.
Nymph of the woods
whose wings take it back to the woods.

Labyrinth.

Song of Awambeh

I am talking while the sun is shining.
I say this looking at the sun.
I cleaned a homestead and you moved in.
You moved in and sent me out.
And I overlooked it
For our fathers say that
The plantain on top of a hill
Is the harvest of the storm.

And now…
You are harvesting bananas,
You are harvesting plantains,
You are harvesting plums,
You are harvesting pears.
I planted them all.
The sun knows I planted them.
You are sitting on everything.
I do not even own a ridge.
I have left everything to you.
Yes, the sun knows I have.
The sun knows I can lick the soil saying this.
And now you want my head.
Know you cannot have your way.
I say this while the sun is shining.
I say this looking at the sun.

They went and got you to be my mate.
Did I say no?
Did I refuse?
When the earth refuses the rain
Where else does it want it to fall?
Can a baby refuse a babysitter?
Where will it find the mouth to say so?

Who has ever refused bearded meat
From being taken to the fire place?
Who has ever refused cocoyam
From being put on the fire?

I agreed that you should enter this compound.
A woman needs others
To join in cooking for a man.
To join in warming his bed,
To join in giving him children,
To join in feeding his pigs,
To join in tethering his goats,
To join in working on his cocoa farms,
To join in working on his coffee farms,
To join in working in his palm bushes.
This is what our mothers tell us.
This is what I was told
The day I left for my husband's compound.
This is what you were told
The day you left for our husband's compound.

When your roots saw water in the compound,
When they found tadpoles beneath the clay,
You sent me out.
You sent me out
The way mucus is sent out of the nose.
You sent me out
The way a dog throws out rot.
You sent me out
The way a stray pig is sent running.

You have hoisted my name on a bamboo.
You have hoisted my name on a palm tree.
May you cut your tongue
Should you want to call my name.

May you cut it and swallow the half.
May goitre block your throat
Should you want to call my name.
May fog cover your brain
Should you want to think about me.
You shall crash headlong from back.
You shall fall, fall,
Except you are harvesting what I did not sow.
I am saying this while the sun is shining.

Marriage is the rain that falls on every woman.
It is banana
The day it fills your pot with pork.
It is bitterleaf
The day it fills your pot with crabs.
It is banana
The day it fills your stomach with beer.
It is bitterleaf
The day it fills your stomach with starch.

Know that
The disease that attacks cocoa pods today
Is the same that will attack coffee beans tomorrow.
Know that
The weevil that eats beans today
Is the same that will eat corn tomorrow.
Know that
The wind that pulls down plantains today
Is the same that will pull down banana tomorrow.
Know that
The potato that is sweet today
Is the same that will be bitter tomorrow.
I am saying this while the sun is shining.
Yes, the sun is shining as I am talking.

Tekwombuo

Thunder has rent the sky.
The flood has brought fish to the banks.
The earth has released its juicy termites.
And here, as elsewhere in the land,
Pots once more steam with joy.

Welcome to this family.
Welcome to this world.
We welcome you in good faith.
You will bring this family joy.

We have come to know who you are, new calf of the herd,
We have examined the leaves on the spider's altar,
The way the *nga'ah* placed them for us to see,
And have seen that you are Tekwombuo,
He who bears no grudge against anyone.

Tekwombuo, you are welcome.
Male child, lone one, you are welcome.
We hope you have come to stay
Like the horn on the snout of the rhinoceros.
We hope you are not the milk tooth meant for the roof.

We have many things for you:
This is your oil;
This is your salt;
This is your wine;
This is your kola;
This is your melon;
This is your chicken.

So stay with us, Alligator, fear of the kingfisher,
So that our fence shall no longer be eaten by termites;
So that giant rats shall no longer dig this compound;
So that hawks shall no longer prey on our chickens;
So that owls shall no longer cry on our roof tops.

We shall look for you a wife.
It is said that a woman is a fig tree.
It will always sprout
When stuck into the ground.
We shall then look for *nda'a*
And stick it into the ground
So that it will grow
And never again, never again,
Will the giant rat ever dig this compound.

This meal has then been prepared
And this crowd fed with it
To welcome you,
To welcome the soldier-ant of the colony,
To welcome the soldier-buffalo of the herd.

Male child, you are welcome.
Welcome to this family.
Welcome to this world.
We welcome you in good faith.
You will bring this family together.

We place *fve'afu* on your forehead,
It will protect you.
We put *Ndindi'* in your mouth,
It will calm you.
Let the man with the owl's eyes
Receive wood ash on the face.
Let the man with the chameleon's mouth

Be served with hot water to drink.
Let the man with the fox's mind
Find thorns on his path.

We place you in the hands of *Ndem-mbo'*,
The moulder of human beings,
And ask that you grow like the baobab,
And shine like the sun.

Angwa

Angwa,
You, once thought to be nuts on a palm tree,
The envy of the chief's wives.
How will they get them for their soup pots
When the chief never climbs the palm tree?

Angwa,
The rose lies
When it claims to be
The queen of flowers.
Does it know you rose every tree?
Does it know you rose the forest?

Angwa,
The sun lies
When it claims to light
The tunnel of life.
Does it know you teach the moon how to shine?
Does it know you teach the stars how to twinkle?

Angwa,
Palm birds claim they can talk
But you give speech to the parrot;
You give rhyme to the nightingale;
You give rhythm to the tam-tam.

Angwa,
The robin claims it is bright
But you give colour to the butterfly;
You give colour to the peacock;
You give colour to the rainbow.

Fresh foliage of the savannah,
Juicy pumpkin of the farm land,
Mother hen of the homestead,
With the sun you rise
As with it you set.
You rise to soothe;
You set to rest.

The Celebration

The mantis's prayer over
Larks sang in joyful elegance
As bees hummed the refrains
And bulls bellowed the bass.
The trumpeting of elephants,
The whistling of birds and
The droning of beetles
Rent the air.

Eagles and hyenas screamed in joy
And the robin and sparrow chirped in approval
As the pig was carted in by the horse
For he was the lion's new pick
To head the farm.

Ants filed pass, millipedes too,
Grasshoppers hopped pass, wrens too,
Frogs leaped pass, rabbits too,
Serpents glided pass, seagulls too,
Owls flitted pass, parrots too,
And asses jogged pass and cats stole pass
As the pig grunted repeatedly in approval.

The tortoise staggered in, asked,
Why the celebration? Why? Why?
When the pig's head was in the lion's mouth?

The grey sky looked on,
The chill breeze blew still,
And trees folded their leaves for the night.

Hunting

The Python caught its prey
It laid in wait
For the poor swine to pass out as faeces
And got killed by soldiers of the ant colony.

The Leopard caught its prey
It prowled on for a bigger catch
Having left the rest of the poor deer
For the vulture's feast.

Tell Me

Bees need flowers for honey
As men need bees for honey.
But do bees kill flowers for honey
As men kill bees for honey?

Who Knows?

The bull sleeps with the cow
As the cock with the hen.
But who knows why
A bull sleeps with another bull,
Or a hen with another hen?
Can their bed ever be one of roses?

Who knows the outcome
When an eagle sleeps with a swallow?
Who knows the outcome
When a vulture sleeps with a sparrow?
Can their bed ever be as smooth as the duck's back?

Green Call

The forest is green when man is green,
The sky is grey when man burns green,
Who knew roses can bud the green
When roses never look green?

Green, green, green as green
Melon is sweet when green.
Green, green, green as green
Traffic flows when lights are green.

Roses yield tons of green
As dung yields hectares of green
Life thrives on green
As elephants do on tons of green.

Green, green, green as green
Melon is sweet when green.
Green, green, green as green
Traffic flows when lights are green.

Green makes yards green,
Green makes waters green,
Green makes the sky green,
Green makes the world green.

Green, green, green as green
Melon is sweet when green.
Green, green, green as green
Traffic flows when lights are green.

Greens make houses green,
Greens make man green,
Greens make life green,
Greens make vision green.

Green, green, green as green
Melon is sweet when green.
Green, green, green as green
Traffic flows when lights are green.

The rose beams when the stem is green,
The stem beams when the rose buds green,
Man beams when the forest is green,
The forest beams when man builds green.

Green, green, green as green
Melon is sweet when green.
Green, green, green as green
Traffic flows when lights are green.

The sky gleams when the earth is green,
The earth gleams when the sky feels green,
The duck gleams when the field is green,
The field gleams when the duck feels green.

Green, green, green as green
Melon is sweet when green.
Green, green, green as green
Traffic flows when lights are green.

Green
Rule
Ensures
Everlasting
Newness.

Green
Rule
Ensures
Everlasting
Newness.

Green, green, green as green
Melon is sweet when green.
Green, green, green as green
Traffic flows when lights are green.

Hawks

Tell me
What runs in your heads
When you kill to live.

I know bees survive on nectar
As maggots do on waste.
But do flowers die after the meal?
Is waste disposal not man's worry?

True, the tarantula's venom
Is the dread of all.
But must your sting finish its colony
Because your young ones must live?
Must they fall for you to rise?
Do ants cross the stream on a straw to break it?

Sure, your kind will say
Man survives on chicken
So too do they need them.
But do they rear fowls as man does?
Are they not harvesting where they have not sown?
Even mushrooms, can one harvest them
On another person's farm?

But know this:
The waterfall awaits the boatman
Who fishes on a sleeping river.

Know that
Mosquitoes live safely till they have gotten wings;
When they grow wings they are closer to their graves.

Know that
Goats do not mourn
When a fox dies.

69

The Mosquito and Us (Remembering BB)

Aedes:
>   I help man with the yellow colour of the rainbow
>   So he may see with the eyes of the fox.

Anopheles:
>   I help man with the heat of the furnace
>   So he may boil to feverish heights.

Culex:
>   I help man with the balloon feet of the elephant
>   So he may walk his path and leave a trail.

Man:
>   You anopheline gnats,
>   Snacking on blood gladdens your hearts,
>   Day light exposes the quills of the porcupine,
>   And so one can tell from those quills
>   Whether it is set for battle or not.
>   But you, weevils in a bag of corn,
>   Darkness conceals your skinny frame
>   And your tubular mouth made a riddle.
>   Help, you say.
>   You help man with the sight of the owl,
>   So he may throw cowries on the diviner's floor.
>   You help man with hemlock,
>   So he may vomit venom on his fellow man.
>   You help man with the viper's bile,
>   So he may put on the buffalo's horns.
>   You help man with the scorpion's sting,
>   So he may take up dwelling in the lion's den.
>   You, whose trail crosses the valley,
>   Know that though several trips to the mud pit
>   Enabled the wasp to build a house,
>   The wasp slept outside when the mud pit dried up.

The Clap

Before the clap
nimbus perched on celestial beams
awaiting the call of parched earth.

After the clap
earth, pregnant after the fall,
awaits the call of life.

Life comes
when the rainbow clothes the sky
for halo to crown the earth.

Life comes
when the fall awakens seeds
for plants to green the earth.

Life comes
when flowers secrete nectar
for bees to sweeten the earth.

Life comes
when the fall greens the fields
for cattle to nourish the earth.

Life comes
when brooks brim their banks
for eels to feed the earth.

The earth rises
when the clap bellows
as with bat chimes it sleeps.

It wakes
when the sun lights the sky
for it to sleep no more.

Revelation

Lions crush herds to survive
As hawks crush chicks to survive.

Sharks crush fish to survive
As cats crush rats to survive.

But the furnace waits for survivors
When ground collapses beneath their feet
As the abattoir waits for cows and goats
At the end of their grass meal.

Glossary

Alung-achaba: A royal dance among the Nweh (Bangwas) of the South West Region of Cameroon with very colourful masquerades.

Alung: One of the eight days of the Nweh week.

Alung-ndeng'a: A type of dance among the Nweh and Mbos of Cameroon. *Alung-ndeng'a* masquerades dance on bamboo tips or staffs that are tied to their feet.

Amiliteh: This is a warrior dance among the Bamilekes and the Nweh of Cameroon. The word *amiliteh* is derived from the French word 'militaire' ('military' in English).

Anzieh-mven: A type of leaf

Bang-mpfen: A type of leaf, red on one side (hence *bang-mpfen*, meaning the red side) and green on the other.

Begang-afu: Medicine men (Singular: *ngan-afu*). *Afu* in Nweh language means medicine.

Begang-ngah: This means soothsayers or fortune tellers in Nweh language. *Ngah* in Nweh language means fortune telling.

Belem: This means gods or deities in Nweh language.

Bemuiteh: A type of dance among the Nweh.

Corn *fufu*: Food made from corn flour.

Fonship: Derived from the word 'fon', which means 'chief' in the Western grass field region of Cameroon.

Fve'afu: A powder used for traditional blessing in Nwehland.

Kuh-ngang: A type of dance among the Nweh.

Lefem groves: Sacred groves found at the entrances of chiefs' palaces in the Western grass field region of Cameroon.

Mmah: This means 'palace' in Nweh language.

Nda'a: A fig tree planted in the royal courts and the compounds of notables in the Nwehland

Ndem-mbo': One's creator-god in Nweh mythology.

Ndep: Nweh word for a refuge for sorcerers, believed to be in the invisible world.

Ndindi': A kind of fruit that grows in bushes, belonging to the family of *Aframomum pruinosum*, commonly called Alligator pepper, with sweet hard seeds used by the Nweh for benediction.

Nduat: A concoction made from medicinal plants.

Nga'ah: This means 'spider' in Nweh language.

Nkeng: Name of a plant in Nweh language.

Nto'o: Liquid obtained by squeezing leaves of medicinal plants.

Nwoh-Aleh: A clan shrine in Essoh-Attah, one of the clans in Nwehland.

Suesue'a: A type of leaf used by the Nweh to bless newly wedded couples.

Uhuru: The Swahili word for "freedom"